AF484622
by
Nihar Khemani
& Parul Singh

ISBN
Paperback 979-8-89610-798-9
Hardcase 979-8-89673-330-0

be stupid

be dull

be crooked

be average

be free

be true

be sexy

be whatever

be.

In a world where you can *be* anything...

be
kind,

to yourself as well.

be
the reason

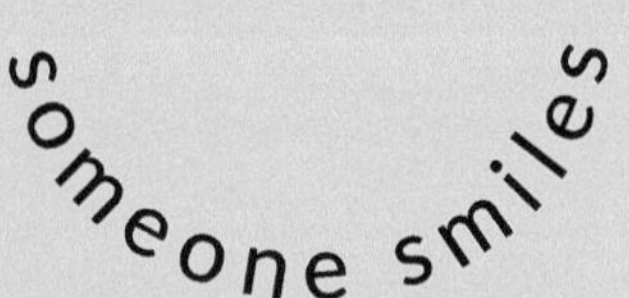

Your lonesome neighbour aunt,
that little girl waiting at the bus stop,
and most importantly, yourself—
just about everyone could do
with a smile.

As easy as it may seem, standing in front of the mirror
and smiling at ourselves for just two minutes is difficult.
Within moments, we start noticing all the imperfections
and become self-conscious.

So, what does it take to bring out that *smile*?
To allow ourselves and others the much-needed grace?

To be enough or
to have enough
is a decision,
<u>not</u> a matter of choice.

Contentment is a life skill.
So lost, yet so imperative,
that the tiniest of amounts
brings with it enormous
learning.

To be content in life
does not mean stopping
our aspirations from
seeing the light of the day,
but rather, to value and
be grateful for the things
we already have.

be
Content

Breathe in.

Breathe out.

be Alive

It is easy
to forget how
precious it is to be *alive*.
When we are neck-deep in work
or completely drowned in a multiverse
of pending tasks and demanding folks
all around, the one thing we
overlook is the most basic
requirement for survival:
to breathe.

Take a
scuba diving session
if you haven't, or try holding
your breath for a minute—as a
toddler would in the middle of
a meltdown—and find out
for yourself!

beauty
of an
ordinary
life

Ever considered that the real treasure
lies in the 'blah' of everyday life?
Have you ever thought about making
every day feel different, even when
you are doing the same things?

Try switching up your routine.
Take a different route to work.
Experiment with coffee flavours.
Change the *tadka* in your dal.
Binge-watch a movie on a weekday.
Or simply give your loved ones an
unexpected bear hug.

Embrace the chaos of everyday life
with a sprinkle of spontaneity.
After all, in the spirit of *ichi-go-ichi-e*,
each moment is a once-in-a-lifetime
experience. So why not make it count?

beyond
mundane

You know how you reach
out for familiar, comforting
things when you become
too settled in your routine?

I reached out for a coffee
mug for my usual cuppa.
And as a last minute call,
decided to switch up my
regular coffee routine with
a milk frother. Not only did
I elevate my coffee game,
watching my flat drink
transform into a frothy
delight turned out to be the
most therapeutic feeling
of the day.

You see, it does not have
to be complicated, always.
Sometimes, an act as simple
as this is enough to help us
overcome the mundane.

be
Inspired

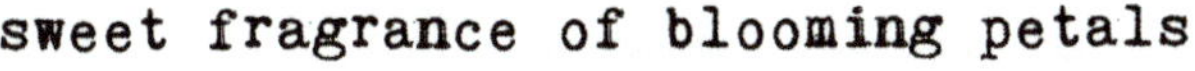

sweet fragrance of blooming petals

patterns of leaves and

shapes of pebbles

untamed wild shrubs and

ripples in puddles

watercolour shades of the sunset sky

shapes of clouds drifting by

If only one could...

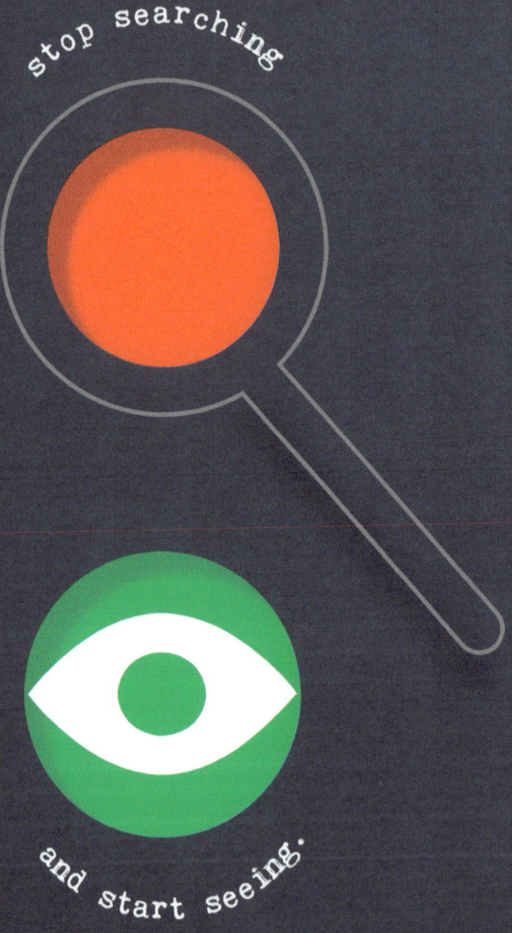

Draw inspiration from
nature for your creations.
Whether in art, cooking,
or simply in the way you
live your life.

Let each sunrise ignite
the promise of a new
beginning, filled with
limitless possibilities
and opportunities to
channel your creativity.

In the vast canvas of
nature, there is no
dearth of inspiration
for those with eyes to
see and hearts open to
receive.

The glitterati
of lights
in the
backyard.

*be*dazzled

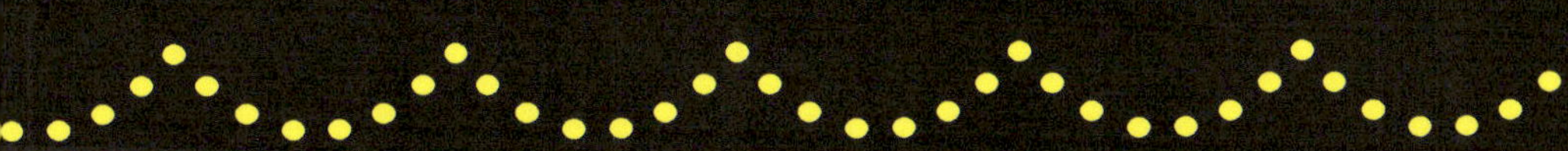

What is the switch that lights up your *mojo*?

Is it something as simple as turning on the lights in the backyard? Bright and covered in glitterati, this could often be the endpoint of your pursuit—as it is for me.

Some nights, I move through the house, methodically turning on a series of fairy lights, a chandelier here, a bedside lamp there. And *tada*! The tiny bulbs of light quite literally fill my soul with mighty brightness. Prosaically forming a smile, as they hang over the fence in my backyard.

be Lit!

What lights you up?

☐ Watching sunrise

☐ Nice hot shower

☐ The whiff of freshly brewed coffee

☐ The earthy scent of rain on dry soil

☐ A warm hug

☐ A genuine smile

☐ Conversation with bestie

☐ Saying goodnight

☐ I love you.

☐ ....

☐ ....

That state of mind
where you are busy doing
nothing. Akin to the feeling that
nudges us to blow soapy bubbles—
that's being *happily unoccupied.*
Because sometimes, it is in these
moments of doing nothing
consequential, that we
experience the magic
of absolute freedom.

be
Happily

un o c c u p i e d

The world we live in,
often leaves little to the
discovery of make-believe.
But would you deny that
make-believe, is what
makes us human?

It is what titillates
those grey cells, to stretch
some more, to live in the moment,
and to enjoy those little things—
lest the state of 'occupied'
takes over.

begin
to procrastinate

It is
all
about
finding
your
balance
between
doing,
and
thinking-of-doing.

Most self-help books or videos tell us not to procrastinate and start 'doing' things, without worrying about the what-ifs and hows.

We said the same thing to ourselves. But it would be appropriate to say that procrastination played a crucial role in the making of this book *(no pun intended)*.

Sometimes, procrastination nurtures creativity. It enables ideas to ferment and bloom into interesting breakthroughs.

Like those seeds you planted in the soil, a memory tucked away somewhere in the back of your mind - only to resurface one fine day, when those dormant seeds sprout, transforming the garden into a beautiful splash of colours.

be Less busy

Whoever said it is important to be busy all the time, forgot to add the equation of prioritization to the problem. Your priorities on any given day might vary—whether it's setting aside time for exercise or taking a break to bake and thus, letting the sweet aromas fill your mind and space.

Busy in the business of being busy?

Only YOU hold the power to prioritize.
Rather, the power to be able to prioritize,
when it is the need of the hour.

It does not have to be everything that
remains to be done. Maybe one little
thing at a time, to add up to the sum!

be Wary
of the bagga*g*e

Saying YES to everything is like trying to carry too many grocery bags at once. Initially, you might take it in your stride, but soon you will find yourself struggling to keep everything from slipping out of your grasp!

Similarly, in life, if you overburden yourself with tasks or favours, you risk dropping important things along the way.

Sometimes, it is necessary to set down a few bags to maintain your balance and to ensure that you are carrying only what's *truly* essential.

Know how much to carry

be
Open

to asking for opinions
to accepting them
to not taking any

Pretty crockery draws me in like a magnet. Each piece so unique and distinctive, its pristine porcelain finish transforms any space almost magically!

I was in my crockery dreamland again at the home decor store when I instinctively turned to a fellow shopper in the same aisle and asked, "Do you think these go well together?"

Pronto came the reply: "Why, young lady, it's been a while since I was asked for an opinion. I will be more than happy to help."

She eagerly helped me pick out the plates that went well together. We walked out of the store in lockstep. I left a happy shopper, and she was simply *happy*.

Its refreshing!

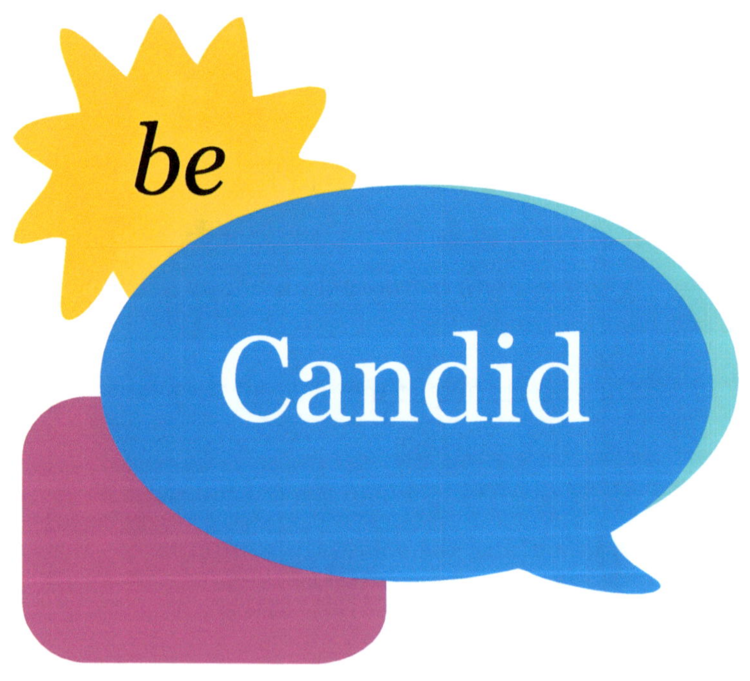
be
Candid

Navigating the fine line
between honesty and
kindness can feel like
walking a tightrope.
If you call a spade a
spade, you might end up
breaking hearts.
But if you sugarcoat
things, you risk losing
the very essence.
Dare to be raw and spill
your heart. You never
know, this could be a
calling to your true,
quirky self.

Be honest but don't be a total heartbreaker.
Be bold but with a touch of kindness.

Leave some wiggle room
for your audience and
give them a sprinkle of
grace; it goes a long way.

Time was not my ally that day.
I had little to no time at hand.
And the mammoth task of finding just the
right footwear to complement my black dress,
lay sprawled in front of me.

I treaded quickly and found myself in a shoe
store, staring at a pair of golden footwear—
just the right shade of gold. One that would
accentuate my dress without taking away
from it. But gold?

"You look like a princess." I swivelled to find
an elderly lady looking at me appreciatively.
"You think so?" was my immediate response.
"Absolutely! Go show them you've got it,"
came the prompt reply.

The decision was made. For me or by me?
I can't say. But my day was made!
And this will forever be *my mark of gold.*

be
gold

be Giving

It was the season, and the malls were overflowing with people wanting to buy gifts for friends and families.

I chose my moment to go to the mall near the end of the day, at almost closing time. The intention was to not wander. Just do the needful and come back with a wallet almost as heavy as it was when I entered the mall.

Going about my chores quickly, I decided to make one visit to a store before the shutters were drawn for the day. Asking for directions to a store while paying at another, I ran to accomplish what I had set out to do.

I just made it to the store when someone tapped my shoulder. I turned around to find the assistant from the previous store waving my wallet in her hand. The relief that washed over my face was evident. In all probability, I would not have found out that I was missing my wallet until I would have reached home (thanks to the tap function on the phone, or shall I say—no thanks).

She handed me my wallet and said, "'Tis the season of giving! How would you feel if you lost this?"
I was rendered speechless, but I am sure my grateful smile said it all to her.

be

Im**per**_fect

How easy it
is to forget
that no one
is perfect,
despite what
we make
the world,
a party to.
The idea
that we need
to be *perfect*,
or else we
are failing
those
around us,
often
makes us
stretch
too thin.

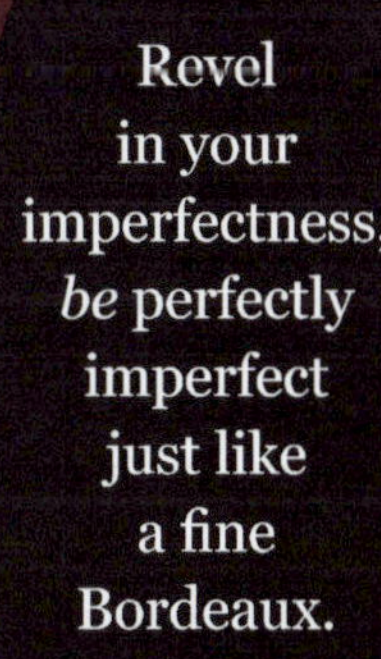

Seeking
acknowledgement,
~~smiles~~, likes,
a fleeting nod,
all of these and more,
are so deeply ingrained
in our being.
To such an
extent that,
unknowingly, we
keep treading the
path that pushes
us to question:
Are we enough?
Are we doing enough?
Are we *doing things*
the way they are
meant to be done?
So on and so forth.

be
Jealous

We live in an age of digital distortion, where every image is filtered and every moment is staged. It is easy to envy the seemingly perfect lives of others—their ideal jobs, happy families, real friends, flawless appearances, wealth, fame, and so much more. Even a simple vacation snapshot on a friend's social media feed can evoke a wistful longing, as we measure it against the backdrop of our own everyday realities.

The grass always looks greener on the other side until you realize it is not the grass that is green—it is the envy-tinted glasses you have been wearing all along! So, ditch those glasses, befriend jealousy, and channelize your inner greenhouse gases to appreciate your own journey. Embrace challenges, and nurture what truly adds value.

As the saying goes,
a lazy person will
always find the easiest
way to get something
done—and often, it's
the smartest way too.
Laziness isn't always
the absence of work;
it can also be an art
of doing just enough
to achieve the goal
with half the effort.

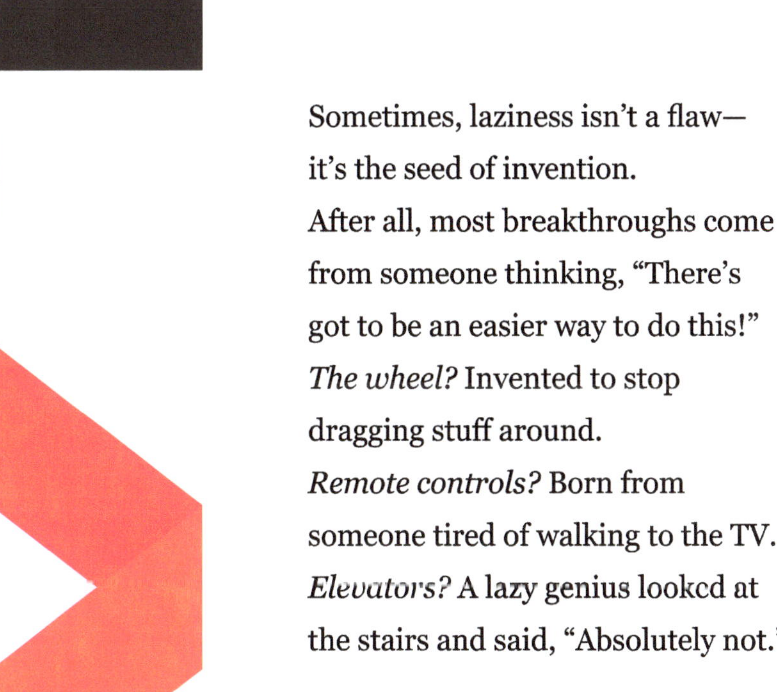

Sometimes, laziness isn't a flaw—
it's the seed of invention.
After all, most breakthroughs come
from someone thinking, "There's
got to be an easier way to do this!"
The wheel? Invented to stop
dragging stuff around.
Remote controls? Born from
someone tired of walking to the TV.
Elevators? A lazy genius lookcd at
the stairs and said, "Absolutely not."

The world doesn't move forward
because of endless effort; it moves
forward because someone decided
there had to be a better way. Who
knows? Your "lazy" idea might be
the next big thing that everyone
else wishes they'd thought of first.

be Yourself

unapologetically

I was in a mad rush to catch the train back home.
So frantic that I practically flew from one stair to
the next, precariously balancing a cup of coffee in
one hand and my heavy office bag in the other.
The bag felt heavy not just because of its contents
but also from the weight of a tonne of withheld
feelings—emotions that had surged through me
during the course of the day but remained unsaid.

I ran up the stairs as a barrage of people descended.
Apologizing every step of the way, in single-minded
pursuit of one goal—making it to the train!

At the topmost step, I mumbled to a lady I came
face-to-face with, "Sorry, I'll just pass."
Prompt came the reply, "Don't be!"
I finally made it to my train, and the bonus was the
smile I couldn't shake off, thanks to the unexpected
generosity.

A simple act of kindness can magically alter our reaction to stressful situations.

In the mad rush of everyday life, even small gestures of compassion can serve as a reminder that we are all in this together.

These moments give us a brief but meaningful break from the chaos. They cut through the noise and offer a moment of calm, helping us shift our focus from frustration to peace.

Prioritizing these moments offers a much-needed sliver of sanity, restoring what we might feel is missing from our lives.

In life's metro station,

amidst the crowd's frenzied dance,

obligations, desires, and fears

each vie for a chance.

Yet, in the chaos,

a whispered truth resounds—

peace is found in slowing down.

Amidst the rush,

a moment to pause and breathe,

to let the clamour fade,

revealing clarity beneath.

For in the quiet,

a profound solace is found.

A serenade of stillness

in life's merry-go-round.

Slowing down is
not for everyone.
Slowing down is
for everyone.
be Slow

hope is
marvelous

It is the grit to look beyond
the obvious and what lies
straight ahead.

be
Hopelessly
hopeful

hope is funny

It is about accepting where
you are graciously, while
still wanting more.

Just like the trees at the
onset of autumn—accepting
their bare look but hoping
to hold on to the leaves
turning into burgundy hues.

hope is
beautiful

For it leaves you in a state of anticipation,
with fervent prayers for all things good—
like the resilient autumn trees holding on
to their burgundy leaves, preparing to brave
the barest state, which will eventually give
way to a brand new season of sprouting.

beneath
the starry skies

I look up to the sky and remind myself that...
I am just a speck in this universe.
And sometimes, that is all it takes for my worries
to suddenly shrink.

I look up to the sky and remind myself that...
Nothing is permanent—
just like the drifting clouds.

I look up to the sky and remind myself that...
Everything is a process.
There are highs and lows, making the silver linings—
sometimes, they are evident, and at others, not so
much, but they are ever present.

I look up to the sky and remind myself that...
I am a part of the greater scheme—
insignificant in the grand scale, yet undeniably
important in the small moments that define my
existence.

Allow the mind to wander
but come back stronger.
Let the body be laid back
but return recharged.
Muster the courage to
ride through the highs
as much as the lows.

Like pebbles on the beach,
battered wave after wave.
Reshaping every time—
yet together,
having endured it all,
they stay put, regardless.

before
you find your success

Failure does not define us.
It helps us become better,
stronger, and kinder.
Life is full of setbacks.
How we get back matters most.
It is ok to feel down.
It is ok to feel let down.
It is ok to not be ok.

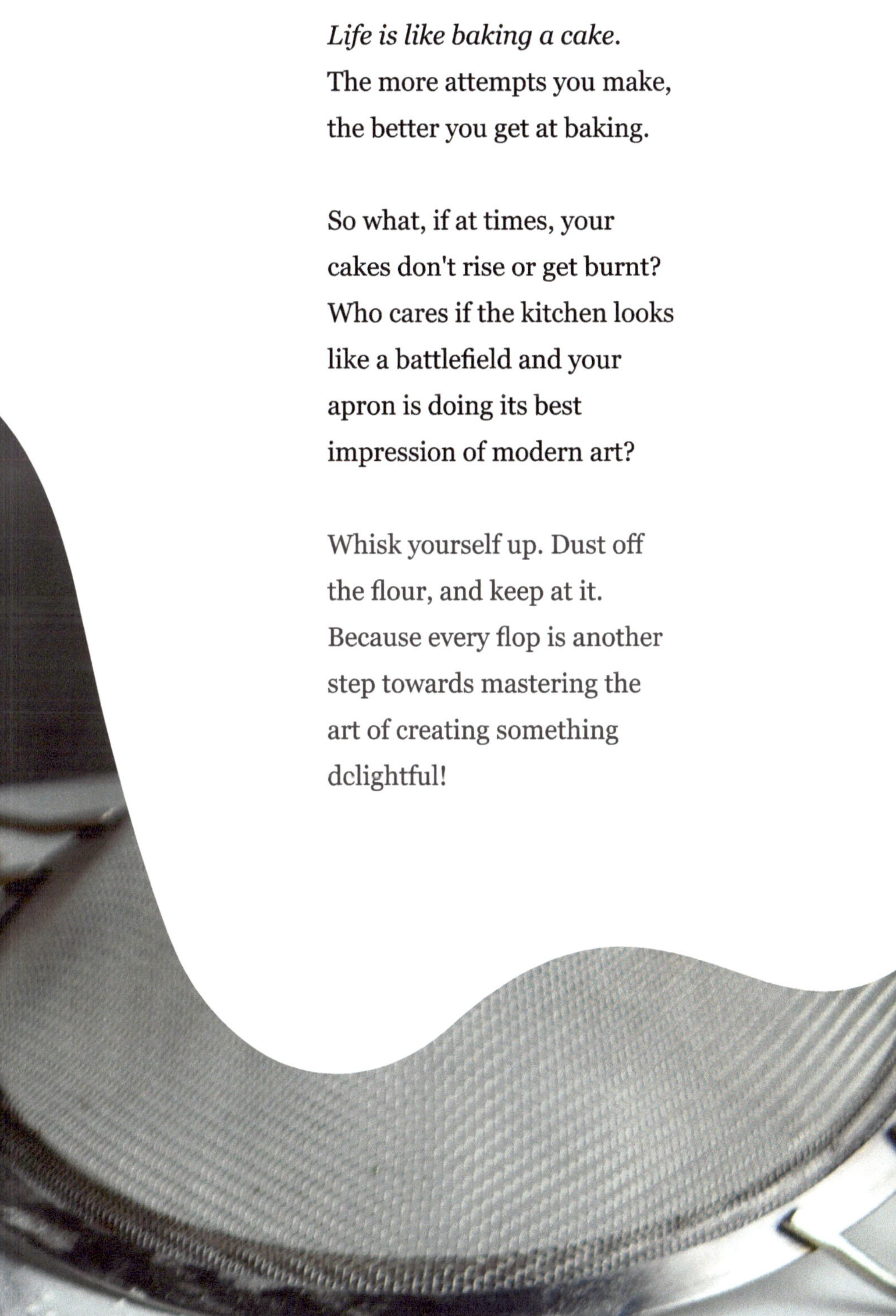

Life is like baking a cake.
The more attempts you make,
the better you get at baking.

So what, if at times, your
cakes don't rise or get burnt?
Who cares if the kitchen looks
like a battlefield and your
apron is doing its best
impression of modern art?

Whisk yourself up. Dust off
the flour, and keep at it.
Because every flop is another
step towards mastering the
art of creating something
dclightful!

be Red
when
you
are
feeling
blue

Strange as it may sound, being
red is just the little lift you need
on days when you're feeling blue.

The hint of a vibrant hue in your
attire, the bright shades of the
evening sky, or that speck of
colour in your stack of papers.
Sometimes, all it takes is a quick
glide of red ink in a sea of blue
to brighten an otherwise dull day.

Let that red remind you to be
bold and forward-looking in your
thoughts and actions. On days
that seem to drag, when everything
feels heavy, and nothing makes
sense, let that speck of red help
you push through.

Red may not always be *red*.
If so, let black be your *red*.

in be

tween

In between is a fleeting space—
a moment of *process*,
a gentle embrace.
In the period of transition,
laugh at the mess, don't fret.
For patience is the key,
and humour your best bet.
Stumble, then find your balance,
in each graceful, steady sway.
While you try to fit in,
let your mind guide the way.

believe

The incessant rain was exactly the downpour my heart needed— a moment to curl up and savour my hot cuppa, letting everything fade away in the soothing rhythm of water droplets peltering on the windowpane. It felt as if the universe conspired to bring me to the place I needed to be at, most.

There are days when I long to close my eyes and find myself exactly where my heart yearns to be. And then, there are days when where I am, in that very moment, becomes my happy place.

What sets one apart from the other is the sense of contentment — whether found in the present, the future, or, more often, in the memories of the past. Allow limiting beliefs to fall away and create space for your dreams to take the lead - for it is all in the belief.

Being close, we so often are:

to a treasure chest of smiles,

to savouring little moments of joy,

to holding on to hope,

to finding strength,

to losing faith and

finding it again.

All this, while discovering

who we truly are.

Realizing that the essence of

our journey lies not in arriving—

but in the becoming,

in the almost-there.

being
close

Our human essence lies not in
arrival, but in being *almost there*.
We are wanderers on our way.
Our journey, a series of impending,
anticipated arrivals.

After all, what makes the rainbow
beautiful is not the pot of gold at
its end, but the arc of its journey—
between here and there, between
now and then, between where we
are now and where we want to go.

In the notion of closeness lies the
rich taste of life, revealed through
a unique experience that shapes
each step, gradually framing the
destination itself.

bespoke
relationships

If only I could…

meticulously craft the threads of my relationships. Shaping each interaction to fit the contours of my heart, intertwining them with my cherished values and dreams.

If only I could…

weave boundaries that honour my needs and desires. Embroider traditions and rituals, adding intricate patterns of meaning to the fabric of my connections.

If only I could…

knit a quilt of love and belonging with threads of heartfelt conversations that envelop me in warmth and love, reminiscent of the tender embrace of my grandmother's bespoke masterpieces.

If only I could

I love gifting and have always found utmost joy in shopping for friends and family—all the more so when there is a trip back home on the horizon. It was that time of the year again, and I was desperately wanting to send something for my mother—a simpleton who rarely speaks her desires out loud. She did on this particular occasion, so I had to make it happen.

In the garment store, my eyes rested on just the perfect cardigan for my mother. It was a style that I know she had never worn. I have been diligently proposing things that she may have been apprehensive about trying on but are *á la mode*, and I have seen some success.

While browsing through the aisles, I had spotted an
elderly woman, about my mother's age, with the
same petite frame, sifting through cardigans. In the
spur of the moment, I asked her if she could try on
the cardigan I intended to buy for my mother.

She did.

It looked great, and I went ahead with my purchase
while thanking her profusely for her generosity.
All she had to say, with a smile that lit up her face,
was, "It's no problem, honey. The world needs so
much more love."

Be-loved is such an underrated word, often associated
with familiar objects, surroundings, or people.
Ever tried tying it to experiences?
I did not—until I had this
experience and could not
help but place it in the list
of *be loved.*

befriend
your oldies

I go back home to many things, but the one feeling that is incomparable is the warm embrace of grandma. Her smile radiates with unmatched joy, and the twinkle in her eyes when she sees me feels truly special. Her gaze follows me silently, cherishing every moment and storing each glance and action in the depths of her loving, experienced heart.

It is never a matter of choice to spend time with her.
It is just as natural as the laughter we share over the
wisdom she bestows on me from experience. Our love
flows like a steady river, with the friendly banter that is
so special and unique in it's own accord. It is filled not
with the weight of expectation, but with the warmth of
friendship that kindled when I was all but a tiny tot.

beyond
the foster smiles

Beyond the foster smiles,
lies a world unseen,
where joys and sorrows
quietly convene.
In shadows cast by
the masks we wear,
emotions linger,
waiting to go bare.
Each fleeting smile,
a veil for tears untold.
Embracing sadness,
until it unfolds.
For in the depths,
true smiles
find their way—
through tears and frowns,
they come to stay.

be Around

for those around

As one climbs the ladder of age, the landscape of life can gradually transform into a solitary path, especially after losing a life partner.

I have often mused to myself that my friend shares a warm connection with her elderly neighbour. Never realizing that it is because this friend makes an extra effort to know the neighbour. For instance, at our latest soiree, she wouldn't stop leaning over from where she was perched, trying to catch the eye of the old lady who had just stepped out of the car across the road.

As soon as their eyes met, my friend quizzed, "Your legs are getting stronger, eh? You're able to drive now?" The frown lines on the lady's face were quickly replaced by a warm smile, lit with appreciation and gratitude. And I couldn't help but reflect that, while her pain may not have subsided, her solitude was now enveloped in a heartwarming smile.

We always
behold
to see
or observe
something
remarkable.
The moment
is often
interlaced
with a sense
of awe.

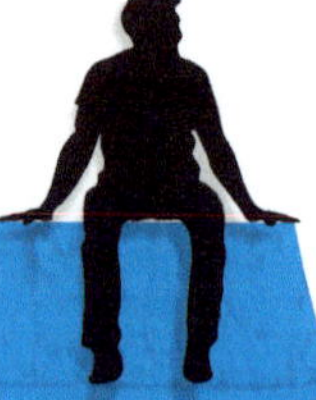

behold

those conversations

But what about daily chit-chats and asks for suggestions on seemingly unimportant things? The frustration of pouring your heart out to someone physically present but emotionally absent is similar to the exasperation of staring at a webpage, waiting to load.

Often, I turn this annoyance into a light-hearted smirk, mumbling to myself that I should write a guide titled *'What Not to Do While Your Partner Is Talking.'*

Why is it so difficult to behold random conversations?

DON'T ┈┈┈┈┈

- Question
- Compare
- Judge
- Suggest
- Preach

It takes courage to ask for 'help'.
There are times when
people are in pain, grieving
or feeling just a little low.
A hug, a patient and calm outlook,
listening with intent or a small note,
letting one choose their moment—
is all that they may be seeking,
knowingly, and sometimes
unknowingly so.
Step back and just *be* there.
Little things make a big difference.

be
There

Sometimes that's all that matters.

be Anchored

Imagine yourself as a grand ship sailing the vast ocean of life. The sea may toss you around with waves of criticism or carry you gently with breezes of praise. You might find yourself battling storms of challenges or cruising through calm, serene waters.

Finding the right anchor is like choosing your favourite snack — everyone has their own preferences. It could be the unwavering support of family and friends, your value system, or the habits and lifestyle you hold dear.

Your strength comes from your anchors, firmly rooted in your own truth. Discover what keeps your ship from drifting into a sea of chaos.

To stay unfazed is to keep your course steady, using your anchor to maintain direction. As you navigate, let your inner strength steer you—like a ship that refuses to let a little water in its hull slow it down. After all, even pirates learn to laugh at a good storm!

belong

to a place called

home

While the notion of home often conjures images of brick and mortar, its true essence lies in the warmth of shared laughter, the comfort of unconditional acceptance,
the embrace of kindred spirits, the familiarity of traditions, and the knowledge of being valued.

It is like your favourite sweatshirt-comforting, familiar, and just right. Home is where our hearts settle, wrapped in the cozy embrace of love and understanding.

What does home feel like for you?

....

~~The End.~~
The Beginning.

Acknowledgements

Brijesh & Ryan
Amit & Aadi
Our parents

*for all the love that makes
our life's landscape bright
and beautiful.*

Paul Rand &
Alan Fletcher

*legends whose work has
inspired our designs.*

You, our
dear reader

*and now our co-passenger
on this journey.*

Most importantly,
to **each other,**

*for nagging and pulling
each other across continents.
Through time differences
and multiple commitments,
we somehow managed to
put this book together after
four years of back and forth!*

The Authors

Nihar and Parul—two no-nonsense women navigating the highs and lows of life with their unique viewpoints. With two decades of professional experience, they infuse their passion for storytelling and artistic flair into everything—from experimenting with recipes, to arranging and rearranging knick-knacks, to curating quirky treasures discovered on random adventures...because sometimes, the most beautiful things happen every day.

Together, they've whipped up this refreshing book—a lively mix of life lessons and insights, infused with a poetic dash of everydayness. With each page crackling with its own charm and character, this book is perfect for anyone seeking a platter of emotions akin to a roller coaster ride of nostalgia.

This shared collective is a treasure trove
of life lessons and everyday wisdom,
with just the right amount of poetic flair.

It is wrapped cozily in a four-year
hug of love — perfect for when you need
a good laugh, a little reflection, and
a whole lot of warmth.

www.ingramcontent.com/pod-product-compliance
Lightning Source LLC
Chambersburg PA
CBHW040853110726

48005CB00001B/54